W9-BIC-875

-in as in
twin

Kelly Doudna

Consulting Editor Monica Marx, M.A./Reading Specialist

Published by SandCastle™, an imprint of ABDO Publishing Company, 4940 Viking Drive, Edina, Minnesota 55435.

Printed in the United States.

Credits
Edited by: Pam Price
Curriculum Coordinator: Nancy Tuminelly
Cover and Interior Design and Production: Mighty Media
Photo Credits: Comstock, Corbis Images, Eyewire Images, Hemera, PhotoDisc, Stockbyte

Library of Congress Cataloging-in-Publication Data

Doudna, Kelly, 1963-
    -In as in twin / Kelly Doudna.
       p. cm. -- (Word families. Set III)
    Summary: Introduces, in brief text and illustrations, the use of the letter combination "in" in such words as "twin," "begin," "chin," and "pin."
    ISBN 1-59197-238-8
    1. Readers (Primary) [1. Vocabulary. 2. Reading.] I. Title.

PE1119 .D675837 2003
428.1--dc21   2002038635

SandCastle™ books are created by a professional team of educators, reading specialists, and content developers around five essential components that include phonemic awareness, phonics, vocabulary, text comprehension, and fluency. All books are written, reviewed, and leveled for guided reading, early intervention reading, and Accelerated Reader® programs and designed for use in shared, guided, and independent reading and writing activities to support a balanced approach to literacy instruction.

Let Us Know

After reading the book, SandCastle would like you to tell us your stories about reading. What is your favorite page? Was there something hard that you needed help with? Share the ups and downs of learning to read. We want to hear from you! To get posted on the ABDO Publishing Company Web site, send us e-mail at:

sandcastle@abdopub.com

SandCastle Level: Beginning

-in Words

grin

pin

spin

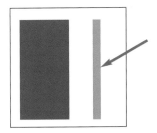

thin

twin

win

3

Linda's pinwheels
make her grin.

The bowler tries to hit
a pin.

Rich takes a spin on
the merry-go-round.

Jim wears a shirt with thin stripes.

Vic has a **twin** brother.

Chris will win the race.

10

Which Twin
Will Win?

Quinn likes to bowl
with his twin, Brin.

Quinn picks a ball
from the bin.

Brin aims at a pin.

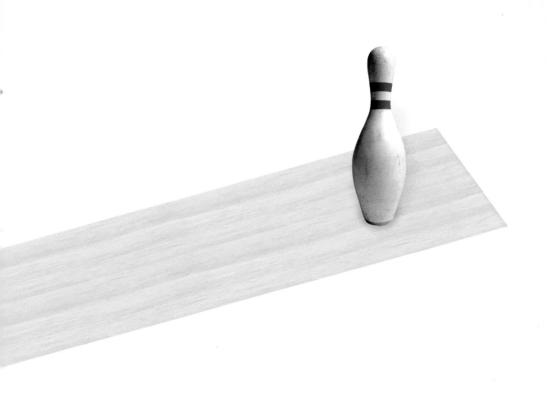

The alley is thin
and so is the pin.

Brin misses the pin.
He rubs his chin.

Quinn has a big grin.
He wants to win!

Quinn hits one pin
and then another pin.

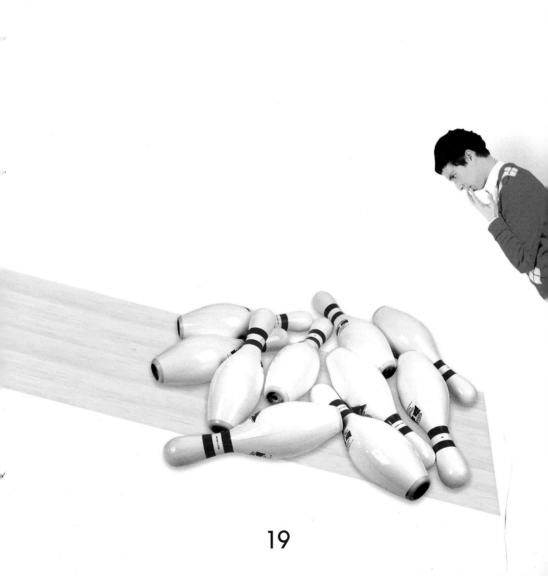

19

Quinn gets
the gold pin
for his win!

The -in Word Family

begin	shin
bin	sin
chin	skin
fin	spin
grin	thin
in	tin
kin	twin
pin	win

Glossary

Some of the words in this list may have more than one meaning. The meaning listed here reflects the way the word is used in the book.

alley   the narrow lane where you roll a bowling ball

bin   container or space used for storing things

bowling   a game in which you try to knock over pins by rolling a heavy ball down an alley

grin   a big, happy smile

pinwheel   a light wheel that is attached to a stick so it can spin in the wind

twin   one of two children born at the same birth

About SandCastle™

A professional team of educators, reading specialists, and content developers created the SandCastle™ series to support young readers as they develop reading skills and strategies and increase their general knowledge. The SandCastle™ series has four levels that correspond to early literacy development in young children. The levels are provided to help teachers and parents select the appropriate books for young readers.

Emerging Readers
(no flags)

Beginning Readers
(1 flag)

Transitional Readers
(2 flags)

Fluent Readers
(3 flags)

These levels are meant only as a guide. All levels are subject to change.

To see a complete list of SandCastle™ books and other nonfiction titles from ABDO Publishing Company, visit www.abdopub.com or contact us at:

4940 Viking Drive, Edina, Minnesota 55435 • 1-800-800-1312 • fax: 1-952-831-1632